Grades PreK–K

Summer Bridge Essentials Backpack User Guide

Summer Bridge ACTIVITIES

Prevent summer learning loss in just 15 minutes a day!

Research findings report about **2 months of learning loss during the summer,** with the highest losses occurring in **math and spelling**.

97% **of teachers** say it's important for students to **practice the skills** they learned in school during the summer.

92% **of teachers** agree that students will be more successful in the long run if they **maintain some form of learning during the summer**.

89% **of parents plan to continue some form of learning with their children** during the summer.

9 out of 10 parents agree that if they knew their children were going to experience summer learning loss, they would **try to prevent it**.

84% **of parents** agree that if children **maintain some form of learning during the summer**, they will be more successful in the long run.

Sources
1. Carson Dellosa Education Summer Learning Survey, December 2017.
2. Research findings report about 2 months of learning loss per student during the summer, the highest losses occurring in math and spelling (http://archive.education.jhu.edu/PD/newhorizons/Journals/spring2010/why-summer-learning/index.html).
3. Summer reading loss is cumulative; these children do not typically catch up in the fall. Their peers are progressing with their skills while they are making up for the summer learning loss. By the end of 6th grade, children who lose reading skills during the summer are on average 2 years behind their peers (http://www.brighthubeducation.com/summer-learning-activities-ideas/78894-how-reading-prevents-summer-learning-loss/).
4. By ninth grade, summer learning loss could be blamed for roughly two-thirds of the achievement gap (http://www.time.com/time/magazine/article/0,9171,2005863,00.html).
5. Teachers typically spend 4–6 weeks re-teaching material that students have forgotten over the summer (Ron Fairchild, Executive Director of the Johns Hopkins Institute for Summer Learning, http://www.whatkidscando.org/archives/whatslearned/WhatIfSummerLearning.pdf).

How to Use Your Summer Bridge Essentials Backpack Materials

Your backpack includes a variety of materials to help your child learn this summer.

- One *Summer Bridge Activities* workbook
- Flash cards
- Four summer reading books from Rourke Educational Media
- One Summer Reading Log (at the back of this User Guide)
- Three monthly calendars (at the back of this User Guide)

Before you begin, consider setting up a summer learning area at home. A dedicated space for learning can help motivate your child, nurture creativity, and improve focus. Show your child that you value learning by creating an inviting space. It should have good lighting and a place for supplies such as pencils, crayons, and extra paper. Have your child make and decorate a special sign for the area.

Follow the guidelines below to make the most of each part of your backpack.

Summer Bridge Activities Workbook
The workbook is the core of your child's summer learning program. It has two pages of fun activities for each weekday of the summer and supports your child's skills in beginning reading, math, basic skills, science, fitness, and character development. Skills your child learned as a preschooler are reviewed toward the beginning of the book. Skills for the year to come are introduced toward the end.

Encourage your child to use the workbook's bonus features. Cut out the flash cards from the back of the book and thread onto a ring or keep in a zip-top bag so you can take them on the go. Let your child use a star sticker to show that each day's activities are complete.

Flash Cards
Use these handy cards to practice important early learning skills. Take them along with you when you travel or run errands. Refer to the resource card in the box for game and activity ideas.

Summer Reading Books
Four high-interest books, specially selected for your child's age level, are included: two nonfiction and two fiction titles. Let these books be the beginning of a summer full of fun, pleasurable reading for your child!

How to Use Your Summer Bridge Essentials Backpack Materials (Continued)

Read the books together, making sure that your child understands all the words. Then, read them again and again throughout the summer. In each book, look for discussion questions as well as tips and suggestions for using the book as a springboard to learning.

Find even more tips for helping your child learn through reading on pages 3–6 of this User Guide. These ideas can be used with any book your child wants to read. They will increase your child's engagement and help maximize the benefit and enjoyment of summer reading.

Summer Reading Log

Find this easy-to-use log on the last page of this User Guide. You may want to detach it and display in a convenient place. Use it to track your child's reading throughout the summer, duplicating the page as needed. You might want to use the log to record progress toward a reading goal, such as reading 20 books over the summer.

Reading for pleasure is one of the best ways for your child to develop thinking skills. Visit your local library often. Make time each day for sharing books together or for your child to look at books independently. Find summer reading suggestions in your *Summer Bridge Activities* workbook beginning on page viii.

Monthly Calendars

The three calendar pages found in the back of this User Guide loosely correspond to the three months of a typical summer vacation. You may want to post each calendar on the refrigerator or in another handy spot.

The calendars include suggested learning activities for each weekday of the summer. Encourage your child to do as many as possible. Aim to spend at least 15 minutes each day on learning activities. This will help your child keep skills sharp and prepare for kindergarten.

You know your child best! Do not hesitate to modify the number or type of activities to fit your child's needs. It's okay to help your child or to take a break and pick up on another day. Use your creativity to make an activity more or less challenging, to extend it through a fun project, or to connect it to your child's life.

Let's get started! Your child is on the way to a summer full of fun and learning!

SUMMER READING GUIDE: FICTION

Reading fiction is a great way for your child to use their imagination, to exercise thinking and problem-solving skills, and to grow in their ability to empathize with people who are different from them.

Find suggestions for fiction books that match your child's age level and interests in your *Summer Bridge Activities* workbook beginning on page viii.

Use the ideas in the following sections to extend engagement and learning for any fiction book your child wants to read.

BEFORE READING

Preview
Look at the book and build excitement for reading it. Read the title and talk about the picture on the cover. Read the blurb on the back of the book together. Pick up the book and flip through it. What pictures look especially interesting? How many words are on each page?

Connect
Ask your child to think about how the story might relate to their own life experiences. Is the main character older or younger than them? Are the places shown familiar or unfamiliar? Are the characters likely to encounter any situations that your child has lived through?

Activate your child's background knowledge about the story. For example, if the story is about growing a garden, invite your child to think about their own experiences with helping plants grow.

Predict
Talk about what your child thinks might happen in the story. Challenge your child to provide reasons for their predictions.

DURING READING

Pay Attention to Print
As you read, point to letters and familiar words and ask your child to identify them. Help your child understand that letters make up words and that the words tell the story. Sweep your finger along under the text to help your child understand that we read from left to right and from top to bottom. Choose a few simple words to help your child read by matching each letter to a sound and blending the sounds together.

Stop and Check
When you come to an unknown word, stop reading and talk about what it means. Together, check the surrounding text and the pictures for clues to the word's meaning. You may wish to keep a list of new words your child has learned.

Pause and Predict
Occasionally, stop and talk about the story. What has happened up to this point? What challenges are the characters facing? What decisions does your child think they will make? Encourage your child to provide reasons for their predictions using evidence from the story.

 **SUMMER READING GUIDE: FICTION**

Identify Story Elements

As your child reads and discusses the story, prompt them to use special terms related to fiction.

Who are the *characters* in the story?

What is the *setting* of the story? Is the setting important to the story, or could it happen anywhere?

What *events* in the story happen at the *beginning*, the *middle*, and the *end*?

What *problem* does the main character face? What does the character say or do to solve the problem?

AFTER READING

Check Understanding

Ask questions to check your child's understanding of the story. Ask basic questions (example: How did the giraffe escape from the zoo?) as well as questions that require more complex thinking (example: How did the character feel at the party?). If the book includes questions designed to check reading comprehension, use them with your child.

Discuss

Talk about the story with your child. How did the ending make your child feel? What questions did it raise? Does your child agree or disagree with the main character's choices? Invite your child to remember favorite parts of the story and describe why they are memorable or meaningful. If the book includes discussion questions, use them with your child.

Extend

Encourage your child to extend their enjoyment of a story by connecting it to a fun project, activity, or exploration. Be creative and come up with your own ideas, or try these:

- Make a finger puppet for each character and act out the story.
- Draw a new picture for the story.
- Use blocks or other building toys to represent the story.
- Write and illustrate three important words from the story.
- Make cards that show events from the story. Mix them up, then put them in order to show what happens at the beginning, middle, and end.

SUMMER READING GUIDE: NONFICTION

Reading nonfiction is a great way for your child to gain fascinating knowledge about the world, to exercise critical thinking skills, and to practice reading for information—a skill they will use throughout their lives in an increasingly complex world.

Find suggestions for nonfiction books that match your child's grade level and interests in your *Summer Bridge Activities* workbook beginning on page viii.

Use the ideas in the following sections to extend engagement and learning for any nonfiction book your child wants to read.

BEFORE READING

Preview
Look at the book and build excitement for reading it. Read the title and talk about the picture on the cover. Read the blurb on the back of the book together. Pick up the book and flip through it. What pictures look especially interesting? How many words are on each page?

Predict
Ask your child to tell what they think the book is about. What kinds of facts will the book include? What questions will it answer? Challenge your child to provide reasons for their predictions.

Connect
Ask your child to think about how the topic of the book relates to their own knowledge and experiences. Does the book provide information about a subject they already know a lot about? If so, what new things are they hoping to learn? Does the subject involve people, places, or things that are unfamiliar? If so, what are they hoping to learn?

Whether the topic is familiar or brand-new, activate your child's background knowledge about it. For example, if the book is about fire trucks, invite your child to remember when they saw a fire truck and what it looked like and sounded like.

DURING READING

Pay Attention to Print
As you read, point to letters and familiar words and ask your child to identify them. Help your child understand that letters make up words and that the words give the information. Sweep your finger along under the text to help your child understand that we read from left to right and from top to bottom. Choose a few simple words to help your child read by matching each letter to a sound and blending the sounds together.

Stop and Check
When you come to an unknown word, stop reading and talk about what it means. Together, check the surrounding text and the pictures for clues to the word's meaning. You may wish to keep a list of new words your child has learned.

SUMMARY READING GUIDE: NONFICTION

Pause and Predict
Occasionally, stop and talk about the book. What questions about the topic have been answered so far? What questions are still unanswered? What information does your child think is coming up next? Encourage your child to provide reasons for their predictions using evidence from the book.

Identify Important Information
As your child reads and discusses the book, prompt them to use special terms related to nonfiction.

What is the *main idea* of the book? What does the author most want you to understand and remember?

What *facts* are provided to support the main idea?

Does the book have photographs or pictures with *captions*, words in *bold*, a *table of contents*, chapter and section *headings*, or a *glossary*? How do these features help you use the book and understand the subject?

AFTER READING

Check Understanding
Ask questions to check your child's understanding of the book. Ask basic questions (example: How many planets are in our solar system?) as well as questions that require more complex thinking (example: How are a squirrel and a rabbit alike?). If the book includes questions designed to check reading comprehension, use them with your child.

Discuss
Talk about the book with your child. What did your child learn about the subject? What do they still want to know? How could they find the answers to their questions? Challenge your child to give three facts and three opinions about the topic, making sure to distinguish between fact and opinion. If the book includes discussion questions, use them with your child.

Extend
Encourage your child to extend their enjoyment of a book by connecting it to a fun project, activity, or exploration. Be creative and come up with your own ideas, or try these:

- Create a short video about the book.
- Draw pictures or simple charts to show information from the book.
- Write a song about facts from the book.
- Explain to a friend or family member what you learned from the book.
- Visit a museum or other site to learn more about the topic.

Section 1 Calendar

This calendar shows suggested activities for each weekday in the first month of summer vacation. Don't forget to log your reading in your Summer Reading Log!

Day 1	Day 2	Day 3	Day 4	Day 5
Complete Day 1 workbook pages. Complete the MONTHLY GOALS section of your workbook. Read! Share something you learned with a friend or family member.	Complete Day 2 workbook pages. Complete a FITNESS ACTIVITY from your workbook. Read! Connect something in the book to something from your life.	Complete Day 3 workbook pages. Use flash cards to keep skills sharp. Read! Draw a picture to go with the book.	Complete Day 4 workbook pages. Complete a CHARACTER DEVELOPMENT activity from your workbook. Read! Write a new word you learned.	Complete Day 5 workbook pages. Complete a BONUS activity from your workbook beginning on page 140. Read! Find a list of sight words. Find as many as you can in your book.

Day 6	Day 7	Day 8	Day 9	Day 10
Complete Day 6 workbook pages. Complete an OUTDOOR EXTENSION activity from your workbook. Read! Connect something from the book you are reading to another book you have read.	Complete Day 7 workbook pages. Show something you did in your workbook to a family member. Read! Predict what will come next in the book.	Complete Day 8 workbook pages. Complete a BONUS activity from your workbook beginning on page 140. Read! Act out something from the story with blocks or toys.	Complete Day 9 workbook pages. Use flash cards to keep skills sharp. Read! Point to three words that you can read on your own.	Complete Day 10 workbook pages. Complete an OUTDOOR EXTENSION activity from your workbook. Read! Draw a picture to go with the book.

Day 11	Day 12	Day 13	Day 14	Day 15
Complete Day 11 workbook pages. Explain to a family member something you want to learn in school next year. Read! Point to and name 10 letters in your book.	Complete Day 12 workbook pages. Use flash cards to keep skills sharp. Read! Choose a favorite page to read aloud to a friend or family member.	Complete Day 13 workbook pages. Complete a FITNESS ACTIVITY from your workbook. Read! Write a new word you learned.	Complete Day 14 workbook pages. Complete a CHARACTER DEVELOPMENT activity from your workbook. Read! Connect something in the book to something from your life.	Complete Day 15 workbook pages. Complete a BONUS activity from your workbook beginning on page 140. Read! Share something you learned with a friend or family member.

Day 16	Day 17	Day 18	Day 19	Day 20
Complete Day 16 workbook pages. Complete an OUTDOOR EXTENSION activity from your workbook. Read! Draw a face and write words to tell what you thought about the book.	Complete Day 17 workbook pages. Complete a READING AND WRITING activity from your workbook on page 139. Read! Connect something from the book you are reading to another book you have read.	Complete Day 18 workbook pages. Use flash cards to keep skills sharp. Read! Predict what will come next in the book.	Complete Day 19 workbook pages. Complete the SCIENCE EXPERIMENT from your workbook. Read! Write a new word you learned.	Complete Day 20 workbook pages. Read! Act out something from the story with blocks or toys. Get a reward! It could be a treat or a fun family activity.

Section 2 Calendar

This calendar shows suggested activities for each weekday in the second month of summer vacation. Don't forget to log your reading in your Summer Reading Log!

Day 1	Day 2	Day 3	Day 4	Day 5
Complete Day 1 workbook pages. Complete the MONTHLY GOALS section of your workbook. Read! Share something you learned with a friend or family member.	Complete Day 2 workbook pages. Complete a FITNESS ACTIVITY from your workbook. Read! Connect something in the book to something from your life.	Complete Day 3 workbook pages. Use flash cards to keep skills sharp. Read! Draw a picture to go with the book.	Complete Day 4 workbook pages. Complete a CHARACTER DEVELOPMENT activity from your workbook. Read! Write a new word you learned.	Complete Day 5 workbook pages. Complete a BONUS activity from your workbook beginning on page 140. Read! Read the same page aloud in three different voices.

Day 6	Day 7	Day 8	Day 9	Day 10
Complete Day 6 workbook pages. Complete an OUTDOOR EXTENSION activity from your workbook. Read! Connect something from the book you are reading to another book you have read.	Complete Day 7 workbook pages. Show something you did in your workbook to a family member. Read! Predict what will come next in the book.	Complete Day 8 workbook pages. Complete a BONUS activity from your workbook beginning on page 140. Read! Act out something from the story.	Complete Day 9 workbook pages. Use flash cards to keep skills sharp. Read! Point to five words that you can read on your own.	Complete Day 10 workbook pages. Complete an OUTDOOR EXTENSION activity from your workbook. Read! Draw a map or chart to go with the book.

Day 11	Day 12	Day 13	Day 14	Day 15
Complete Day 11 workbook pages. Explain to a family member something you want to learn in school next year. Read! Can you find every letter of the alphabet in your book?	Complete Day 12 workbook pages. Use flash cards to keep skills sharp. Read! Find a list of sight words. Find as many as you can in your book.	Complete Day 13 workbook pages. Complete a FITNESS ACTIVITY from your workbook. Read! Write a new word you learned. Draw a picture to show its meaning.	Complete Day 14 workbook pages. Complete a CHARACTER DEVELOPMENT activity from your workbook. Read! Connect something in the book to something from your life.	Complete Day 15 workbook pages. Complete a BONUS activity from your workbook beginning on page 140. Read! Share something you learned with a friend or family member.

Day 16	Day 17	Day 18	Day 19	Day 20
Complete Day 16 workbook pages. Complete an OUTDOOR EXTENSION activity from your workbook. Read! Draw a face and write words to tell what you thought about the book.	Complete Day 17 workbook pages. Complete a READING AND WRITING activity from your workbook on page 139. Read! Connect something from the book you are reading to another book you have read.	Complete Day 18 workbook pages. Use flash cards to keep skills sharp. Read! Predict what will come next in the book.	Complete Day 19 workbook pages. Complete the SCIENCE EXPERIMENT from your workbook. Read! Write three new words you learned.	Complete Day 20 workbook pages. Read! Act out something from the story with blocks or toys. Get a reward! It could be a treat or a fun family activity.

Section 3 Calendar

This calendar shows suggested activities for each weekday in the last month of summer vacation. Don't forget to log your reading in your Summer Reading Log!

Day 1	Day 2	Day 3	Day 4	Day 5
Complete Day 1 workbook pages. Complete the MONTHLY GOALS section of your workbook. Read! Share something you learned with a friend or family member.	Complete Day 2 workbook pages. Complete a FITNESS ACTIVITY from your workbook. Read! Connect something in the book to something from your life.	Complete Day 3 workbook pages. Use flash cards to keep skills sharp. Read! Draw a picture to go with the book.	Complete Day 4 workbook pages. Complete a CHARACTER DEVELOPMENT activity from your workbook. Read! Write three new words you learned.	Complete Day 5 workbook pages. Complete a BONUS activity from your workbook beginning on page 140. Read aloud with a friend! Read different parts in different voices.

Day 6	Day 7	Day 8	Day 9	Day 10
Complete Day 6 workbook pages. Complete an OUTDOOR EXTENSION activity from your workbook. Read! Connect something from the book you are reading to another book you have read.	Complete Day 7 workbook pages. Show something you did in your workbook to a family member. Read! Predict what will come next in the book.	Complete Day 8 workbook pages. Complete a BONUS activity from your workbook beginning on page 140. Read! Use clay or dough to make something from the book.	Complete Day 9 workbook pages. Use flash cards to keep skills sharp. Read! Find a list of sight words. Find as many as you can in your book.	Complete Day 10 workbook pages. Complete an OUTDOOR EXTENSION activity from your workbook. Read! Draw a map or chart to go with the book.

Day 11	Day 12	Day 13	Day 14	Day 15
Complete Day 11 workbook pages. Explain to a family member something you want to learn in school next year. Read! Can you find every letter of the alphabet in your book?	Complete Day 12 workbook pages. Use flash cards to keep skills sharp. Read! Choose a favorite page to read aloud to a friend or family member.	Complete Day 13 workbook pages. Complete a FITNESS ACTIVITY from your workbook. Read! Write five new words you learned. Draw pictures to show their meanings.	Complete Day 14 workbook pages. Complete a CHARACTER DEVELOPMENT activity from your workbook. Read! Connect something in the book to something from your life.	Complete Day 15 workbook pages. Complete a BONUS activity from your workbook beginning on page 140. Read! Share something you learned with a friend or family member.

Day 16	Day 17	Day 18	Day 19	Day 20
Complete Day 16 workbook pages. Complete an OUTDOOR EXTENSION activity from your workbook. Read! Make a list of books you have read. Draw a face beside each one to tell how much you liked it.	Complete Day 17 workbook pages. Complete a READING AND WRITING activity from your workbook on page 139. Read! Write five important words from the book.	Complete Day 18 workbook pages. Use flash cards to keep skills sharp. Read! Predict what will come next in the book.	Complete Day 19 workbook pages. Complete the SCIENCE EXPERIMENT from your workbook. Read! Tell someone what book you think they would like.	Complete Day 20 workbook pages. Read! Act out something from the story with blocks or toys. Get a reward! It could be a treat or a fun family activity.

Summer Reading Log   Name:_____

Date	Title of Book	Number of Minutes Read	Adult Initials

Summer Bridge Essentials User Guide PK–K

REMWIP-0192